Oils (Just a Bit) to Keep Your Body Fit

to Miss Mac Ivor, my fifth-grade teacher
in Rocky River, Ohio

—B.P.C.

to my best friend, Tristan,
with whom I've shared so many culinary
discoveries (and much much more)...

—M.G.

Oils:
fats that are
liquid at room
temperature

Oils (Just a Bit) to Keep Your Body Fit

What Are Oils?

by Brian P. Cleary

illustrations by Martin Goneau

consultant Jennifer K. Nelson, Master of Science,
Registered Dietician, Licensed Dietician

M Millbrook Press • Minneapolis

An oil is a type of fat
that's liquid when not frozen.

The ones that are the best for you

must carefully be chosen.

Though oil's not a food group, you'll need some in your diet.

Fish and nuts and even plants
are often what supply it.

Foods like almonds,

olives,

avocados,

pumpkin seeds,

salmon, trout, and peanuts

healthfully fulfill your needs.

Why do we need oils?
They can help our bodies grow,

protecting vital organs
as they give our hair a glow!

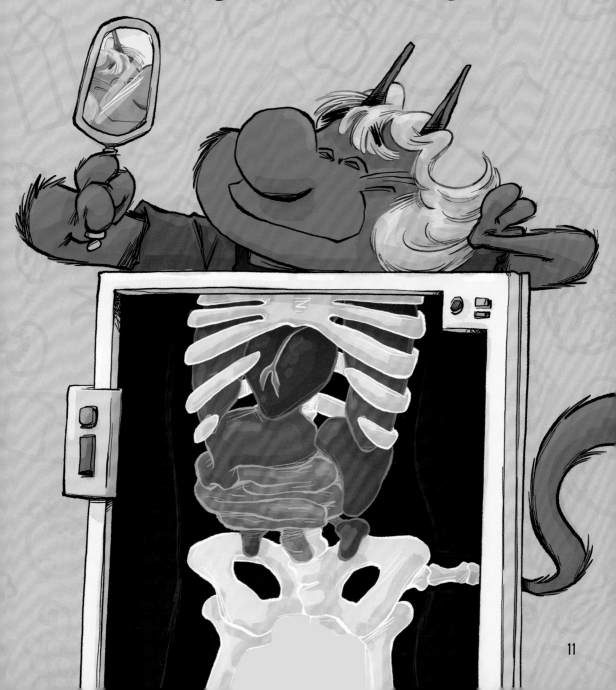

Oils have fatty acids,
    a nutrient that serves

to give us healthy skin and hearts

and strengthen brains and nerves.

These acids link with vitamins
to enter all our parts.

Different types of oils abound:
Soybean oil is one

and cottonseed and olive oils—
the list has just begun!

Oils made from sunflowers,

corn and safflower too,

18

canola,

fish,

and nuts

are all the healthiest for you.

The labels list nutrition facts to keep us all from guessing!

Another food that's mostly oil?

That mayonnaise that you spread,

and **margarines** with no trans fats
you put on rolls
or bread.

Oil can make food tastier when small amounts are added.

But too much fat can make us look

like all our clothes are padded.

How much oil is good for us?
The experts tell us that

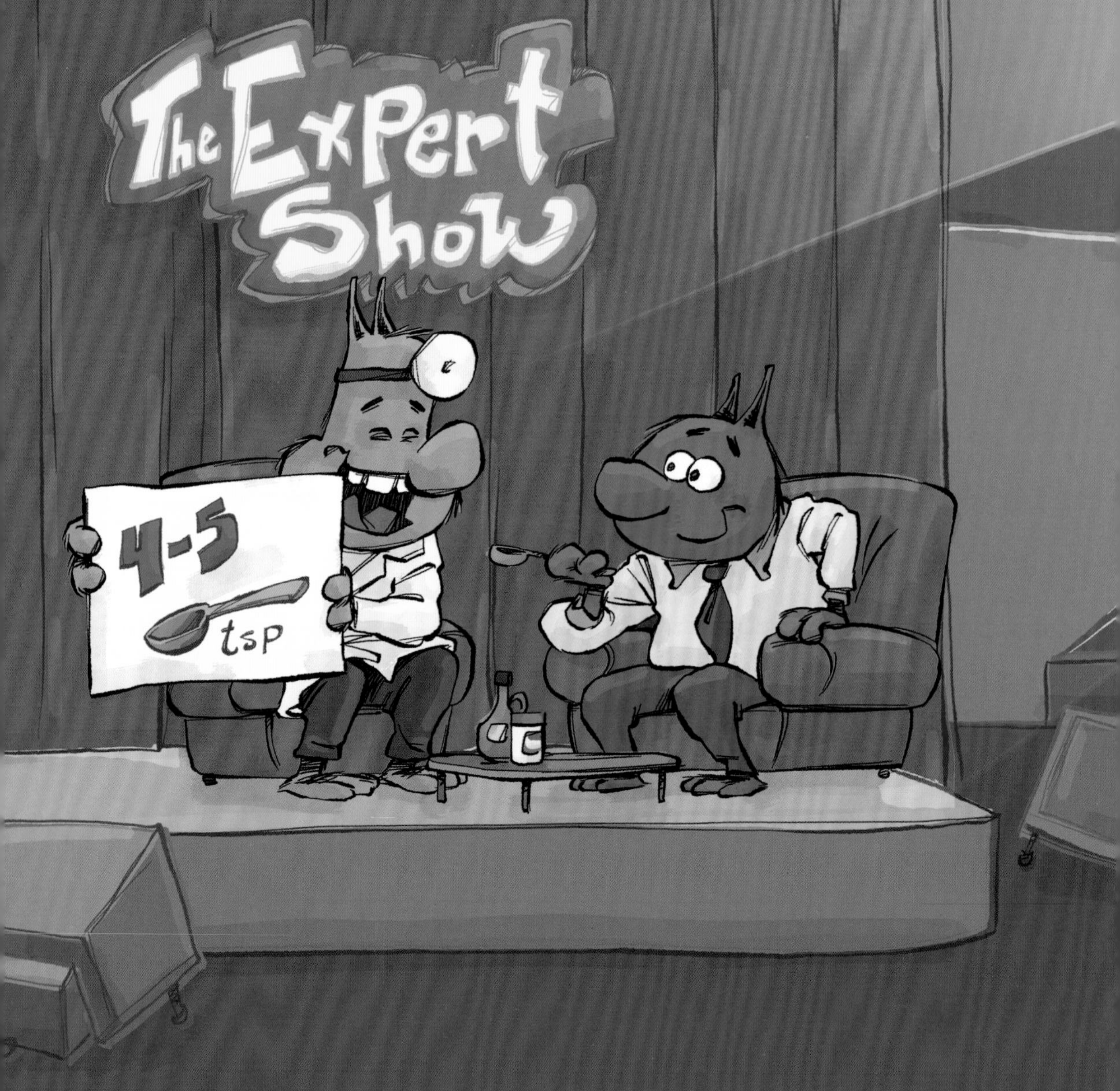

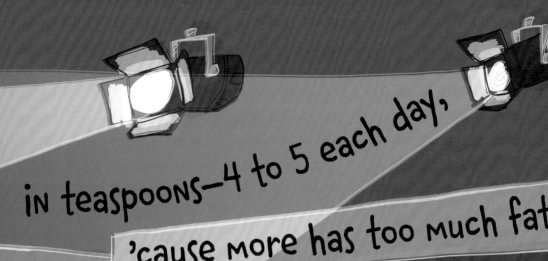

in teaspoons—4 to 5 each day,
'cause more has too much fat.

to eat these in the smart amounts?
"Oil" bet that you can!

So what are oils?
Do you know?

You should eat no more than 4 to 5 teaspoons of oil every day. The exact amount depends on your age and how much exercise you get. To figure out the right amount for you, visit www.mypyramid.gov and click on MyPyramid Plan.

Note: 1 tablespoon of oil
is equal to 3 teaspoons of oil.

2 tablespoons Thousand Island
dressing has 2 1/2 teaspoons of oil.

1/2 medium avocado has
3 teaspoons of oil.

2 tablespoons peanut butter*
has 4 teaspoons of oil.

1 tablespoon mayonnaise has
2 1/2 teaspoons of oil.

1 ounce of almonds* (about 20)
has 3 teaspoons of oil.

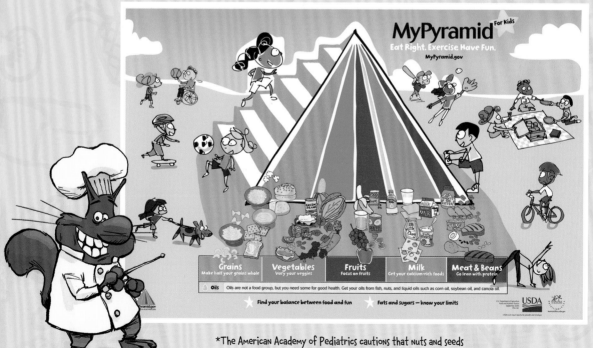

*The American Academy of Pediatrics cautions that nuts and seeds
may be a choking hazard for children under the age of 4. Peanut
butter may be a choking hazard for children younger than 2.

This book provides general dietary information for children ages 5–9 in accordance with the MyPyramid guidelines created by the United States Department of Agriculture (USDA). The information in this book is not intended as medical advice. Anyone with food allergies or sensitivities should follow the advice of a physician or other medical professional.

Find activities, games, and more at www.brianpcleary.com

ABOUT THE AUTHOR, ILLUSTRATOR & CONSULTANT

BRIAN P. CLEARY is the author of the Words Are CATegorical®, Math Is CATegorical®, Adventures in Memory™, Sounds Like Reading®, and Food Is CATegorical™ series, as well as several picture books and poetry books. He lives in Cleveland, Ohio.

MARTIN GONEAU is the illustrator of the Food Is CATegorical™ series. He lives in Trois-Rivières, Québec.

JENNIFER K. NELSON is Director of Clinical Dietetics and Associate Professor in Nutrition at Mayo Clinic in Rochester, MN. She is also a Specialty Medical Editor for nutrition and healthy eating content for MayoClinic.com.

Millbrook Press
A division of Lerner Publishing Group, Inc.
241 First Avenue North
Minneapolis, MN 55401 U.S.A.

Website address: www.lernerbooks.com

Library of Congress Cataloging-in-Publication Data

Cleary, Brian P., 1959–
    Oils (just a bit) to keep your body fit : what are oils? / by Brian P. Cleary ; illustrations by Martin Goneau ; consultant Jennifer K. Nelson.
        p.   cm. — (Food Is CATegorical)
    ISBN: 978-1-58013-592-4 (lib. bdg. : alk. paper)
    1. Oils and fats, Edible—Juvenile literature. 2. Fatty acids—Juvenile literature. I. Goneau, Martin, ill. II. Title.
TX407.O34C53 2011
664'.3–dc22   2009046349

Manufactured in the United States of America
1 – PC – 7/15/2010